South Lanark[shire]

CW00386516

Abington, Ashgill, Biggar, Blackwood, Carl[uke]
Carstairs Junction, Coalburn, Douglas, For[th]
Lanark, Larkhall, Law, Lesmahagow, [Rigside]
Strathaven, West End

Contents

Key to Maps .... Back	Carnwath 18	Lanark Index 20
Legend 10	Carstairs 18	Larkhall 3
Abington 30	Coalburn 28	Law 1
Ashgill 9	Douglas 28	Lesmahagow 23
Biggar 29	Forth 8	Rigside 27
Blackwood 19	Glassford 7	Stonehouse 13
Carluke 15	Kirkmuirhill 19	Strathaven 11
Carluke Index 17	Lanark 21	West End 7

LEGEND

'A' Road	A 123
Bowling Green	●
Bridge Height	10'3"
Bus Station	
Car Park	Ⓟ
Caravan Site	
Cricket Ground	
Fire Station	
Football Ground	●
Golf Course	
Hockey Pitch	✕

Hospital	H
Information Office	ⓘ
Industrial Estate	
BP, Shell etc — Petrol/Diesel	
Railway Station	⇌
School/Education	
Supermarket	
Swimming Pool	
Tennis Court(s)	

ISBN 1 86097 015 X   EDN1 PUB496MVN

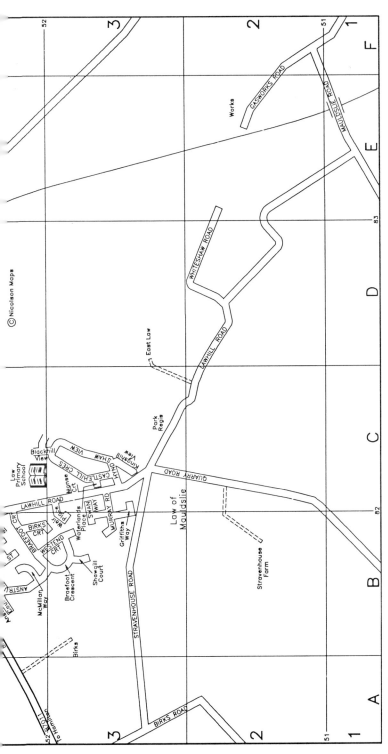

LAW

AIRDRIE ROAD	E5
ANSTRUTHER CT	B4
ANSTRUTHER ST	B4
ASH GROVE	B5
ASHFIELD ROAD	B5
BEECH GROVE	B5
BIRKS COURT	B4
BIRKS ROAD	A3
BLACKHILL VIEW	C4
BLUEKNOWES ROAD	A4
BRACKENHILL RD	C5
BRAEFOOT COURT	B4
BRAEFOOT CRES	B3
BROWNLEE ROAD	B4
BUCHANAN DRIVE	C5
CARMICHAEL ST	B4
CARMICHAEL WAY	B4
CASTLEHILL CRES	C3
CEDAR GARDENS	B5
DOBBIES COURT	C5
GALBRAITH CRES	C5
GASWORKS ROAD	E2
GREENKNOWE DRIVE	B5
GRIFFITHS WAY	B3
HAWTHORN GROVE	B5
HAZEL GROVE	B5
HYNDSHAW VIEW	C3
KINGSHILL VIEW	C3
LAWHILL ROAD	C4
LAWHILL ROAD	D2
LAWMUIR ROAD	B4
MANSE COURT	C3
MAULDSLIE DRIVE	C5
MAULDSLIE ROAD	E1
MCMILLAN WAY	B4
MUIR STREET	B5
MURRAY ROAD	B3
PATTERSON DRIVE	C5
QUARRY ROAD	C2
SHAWFIELD CRES	B4
SHAWGILL COURT	B3
STATION PLACE	C5
STATION ROAD	C5
STATION ROW	C5
STRATH CARRON	C4
STRATH DEARN	C4
STRATH ELGIN	B4
STRATH HALLADALE	C4
STRATH NAIRN	C4
STRATH NAVER	C4
STRATHPEFFER	B4
STRAVENHOUSE RD	B3
SWAN WAY	C3
WATERLANDS PLACE	B3
WATERLANDS ROAD	D5
WEIR PLACE	B3
WESTEND COURT	B3
WHITESHAW ROAD	D2
WILDMAN ROAD	C5
WISHAW ROAD	C7
WOODLANDS AVE	B5

© Nicolson Maps

LARKHALL

ABBEY WALK (12)	D6	BANNOCKBURN DRIVE (24)	F3
ABBOTSFORD AVE	C3	BAREFIELD ST	C6
ACADEMY STREET	C5	BEATON STREET	B6
AFTON STREET	E4	BEECH AVENUE	F4
ALBA WAY	E4	BEECH TERRACE	D3
ALBANY WAY (9)	D6	BEECHWOOD	C7
ALBERT DRIVE	D4	BEMERSYDE PL	C3
ALLOWAY ST (4)	F4	BERTRAM STREET	E3
ANNBANK STREET	B5	BIRCH GROVE	C7
ANTRIM LANE	D6	BIRKS ROAD	D1
ARGYLL GDNS	D5	BLAIR ATHOLL DRIVE (22)	F3
ARRAN PATH (19)	F3	BOWMAN FLAT	C5
ASHBURN LOAN	D6	BRACKEN WAY (34)	E2
ATHOLL WAY (18)	F3	BRAEHEAD AVE	A4
AVON PLACE	D1	BRAESIDE LANE (14)	D6
AVON ROAD	C2	BRAESIDE WAY	D3
AVON STREET	B5	BROOM DRIVE	C7
AVONBANK ROAD	A5	BROOMELTON ROAD	A4
AVONBANK WYND	C4	BROOMFIELD ROAD	C2
BAIRD AVENUE	D2	BROOMHILL GATE	C4
BALFOUR WYND	D3	BROOMHILL ROAD	C4
BALMORAL PATH (5)	F4	BROOMHILL VIEW	B4
BANK WAY (13)	D6	BROWN STREET	C6
		BRUCE'S LOAN (16)	F3

BRYCE GARDENS	C6	CLYDESDALE ST	C6
BURNBRAE STREET	B5	CORONATION AVE	C2
BURNHEAD ROAD	E4	CORONATION CRES	C2
BURNS LOAN (11)	D6	CORONATION PLACE	D2
BURNSIDE PLACE	D5	CORRIE WAY	D4
CADZOW STREET	C6	COSY NEUK	E3
CALEDONIAN ROAD	C5	COVENANT CRES	D4
CAMERON PATH (29)	F3	CRAIGBANK ROAD	C2
CAMERONIAN WAY (38)	E2	CRAIGBANK STREET	C3
CANDER STREET	D2	CRAIGIE LANE (7)	D6
CARLISLE ROAD	A8	CRAIGMORE WYND (10)	D6
CARLISLE ROAD	D2	CROFT	B4
CARRICK PLACE	D6	CROFT PLACE	B5
CARRICK STREET (9)	F4	CROFT ROAD	B5
CATRINE STREET (11)	F3	CROSSGATES ST	B6
CHARING CROSS	C5	CUILLIN PLACE	E4
CHARLOTTE PATH	C4	DAER WALK	C2
CHERRYHILL VIEW	B4	DAVE BARRIE AVE	B7
CHERRYTREE CRES	C7	DEE PATH	C2
CHESTNUT GROVE	C7	DICKSON ST (32)	F3
CHEVIOT ROAD	E4	DON PATH	C2
CHURCH STREET	C4	DONALDSON ROAD	E3
CLAUDES STREET	C5	DOON STREET (2)	F4
CLEM ATTLE GDNS	D4	DOUGLAS STREET	C6
CLOVE MILL WYND	A5		

DRYGATE STREET	C6	GLENORAN LANE	D6
DUKE STREET	C7	GLENVIEW	B6
DUNCAN GRAHAM ST	D6	GOLF GARDENS	E4
DUNEATON WYND	D2	GOODVIEW GDNS	E4
DUNEDIN ROAD	D3	GORBALS CROSS	C5
EARN GARDENS	C2	GRAY STREET	C6
EAST MACHAN ST	D3	GREENLOAN VIEW	D3
EASTWOOD WAY	D6	GRIER PLACE	B4
ELMBANK DR (39)	E2	GROVE CRESCENT	E4
ELMWAY	C7	HAMILTON ROAD	B7
FAIRHOLM STREET	B6	HAMILTON STREET	C6
FAIRWAYS	E5	HARELEESHILL RD	E4
FERNDALE	C3	HAWICK CRESCENT	C4
FIELD ROAD	D4	HAWTHORN GDNS	E4
FIRBANK AVENUE	D3	HAZELDENE LN (30)	F3
FISHER STREET	D3	HEATH ROAD	D5
FLEMING WAY (17)	F3	HIGH AVON ST	B6
FOREST ROAD	D5	HIGH PLEASANCE	C5
FORTH PLACE	C2	HIGHFIELD ROAD	D5
GALLOWHILL	C4	HILL STREET	C4
GEORGE WAY (8)	D6	HILLCREST VIEW	D5
GILLBANK LANE (10)	F3	HILLVIEW CRESCENT	D3
GLEN AVENUE	C3	HINDSLAND ROAD	D3
GLEN FRUIN DR (25)	F3	HOLM PLACE	A4
GLEN GONNAR ST	C2	HOPE CRESCENT	D5
GLENBURN WYND (1)	D6	HOWARD STREET	E3

HOWIE STREET	D3	LOCHNAGAR WAY (21)	F3
HOZIER LOAN (6)	D6	LOMOND WALK (5)	D6
ISLAY GARDENS	D5	LONDON STREET	C6
JANE COURT	C4	LOVAT PATH (3)	F4
JOHN EWING GDNS	C6	LOW PLEASANCE	D5
JOHN STREET	C4	LYNN COURT	C4
JURA GARDENS	E5	MACHAN ROAD	C4
KARADALE GDNS	C4	MACHAN AVENUE	C5
KATRIONA PATH (28)	F3	MACHANHILL	D4
KEIR HARDIE ROAD	E3	MACHANHILL VIEW	D4
KENSHAW AVENUE	C2	MACMILLAN ST	B4
KENSHAW PLACE	C2	MACNEIL STREET	B5
KING STREET	C5	MACPHERSON HO	C6
LAMMER WYND (37)	E2	MAITLAND BANK	E5
LANARK ROAD	E8	MANOR VIEW	E4
LANDSDOWNE ROAD	E4	MANSE VIEW	D4
LANSBURY TERRACE	E3	MAPLE DRIVE	C7
LAUREL DRIVE	E4	MARGARET'S PLACE	C5
LAUREL LANE (33)	E2	MARGARETVALE DR	C4
LAWRIE WAY (27)	F3	MARSHALL STREET	C5
LINKS VIEW	E4	MARTHA PLACE	D4
LIVINGSTONE GDNS	D5	MASON STREET	E4
LOANING (1)	F4	MATTHEW	
LOANLEA CRESCENT	D3	MCWHIRTER PLACE	D6
LOCH PARK PLACE	C3	MAXWELL PATH (14)	F3
LOCHLEE LOAN (12)	F3	MCCALLUM ROAD	D3

MEADOWHILL ST	D5
MEADOWS AVENUE	D5
MELROSE PLACE	C3
MERRYTON ROAD	B8
MERRYTON STREET	B7
MIDDLETON AVENUE	D2
MILLBURN LANE (6)	F4
MILLBURN PLACE	D2
MILLER STREET	D5
MILLHEUGH	A4
MILLHEUGH BRAE	B5
MILLHEUGH ROAD	A3
MONTGOMERY PL	D4
MONTGOMERY ST	C6
MORGAN STREET	B5
MORRIS STREET (35)	E2
MOSSBLOWN ST	B5
MOSSGIEL LANE (7)	F4
MUIR STREET	C5
MUIRSHOT ROAD	D6
MYRTLE LANE	D3
NAIRN STREET	B4
NESS GARDENS	C2
NETHAN PATH	C2
NEVISON STREET	D4
NIKITAS AVENUE	D1
NORTH STREET	C6
ORCHARD GATE	C4
PARK VIEW	D4
PARKER PLACE	D5
PARKNOCK WAY (4)	D6
PATCHY PARK	C2
PERCY STREET	C6
PITLOCHARY DR (36)	E2
PORTLAND WYND (2)	D6
POWFORTH CLOSE	A5
PRIMROSE AVENUE	C3
PROVOST GATE	C5
PYATSHAW ROAD	D3
QUARRY ROAD	C4
QUARRY STREET	D3
QUEENSDALE AVE	D2
QUEENSDALE ROAD	D2
RANNOCH TERRACE	E3
RAPLOCH ROAD	B5
RAPLOCH STREET	B5
REDHOLME PATH	D3
RIVERSIDE ROAD	C2
ROBERT SMILLIE CR	C3
ROSELEA STREET	D6
ROSEMOUNT LN (31)	F3
ROWANTREE PLACE	F4
ST ANDREWS PTH (26)	F3
ST DAVID'S PLACE	C5
SALTIRE CRESCENT	E4

Larkhall

North

LANARK ROAD

Prince's Lodge

Highlees

To Lanark A72

Tilework Cottage

Sewage Works

Skellyton Wood

adowhill

© Nicolson Maps

1 GLENBURN WYND
2 PORTLAND WYND
3 SIGHTHILL LOAN
4 PARKNOCK WAY
5 LOMOND WALK
6 HOZIER LOAN
7 CRAIGIE LANE
8 GEORGE WAY
9 ALBANY WAY
10 CRAIGMORE WYND
11 BURNS LOAN
12 ABBEY WALK
13 BANK WAY
14 BRAESIDE LANE

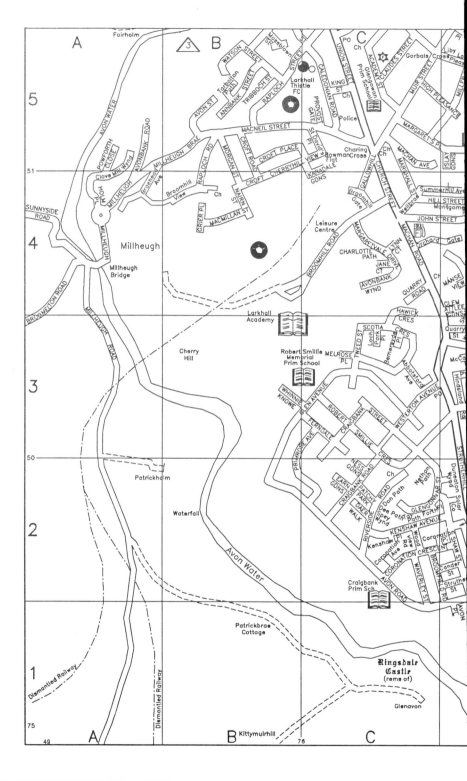

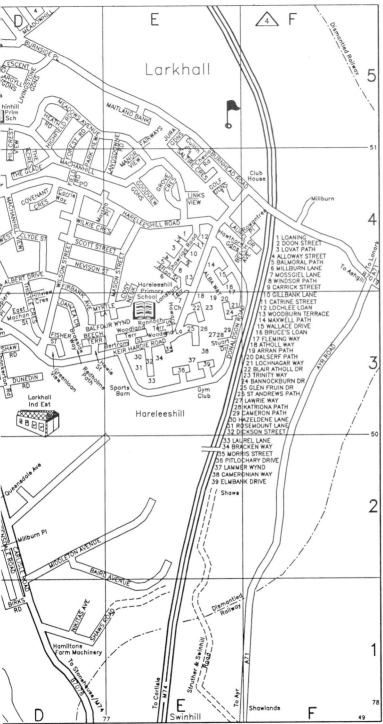

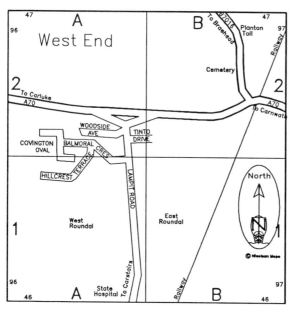

West End

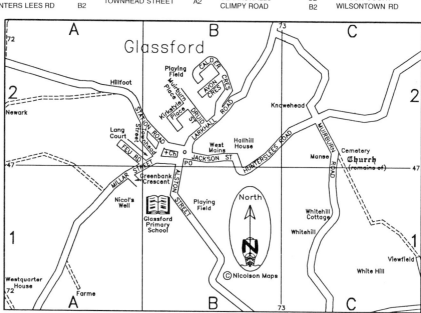

Glassford

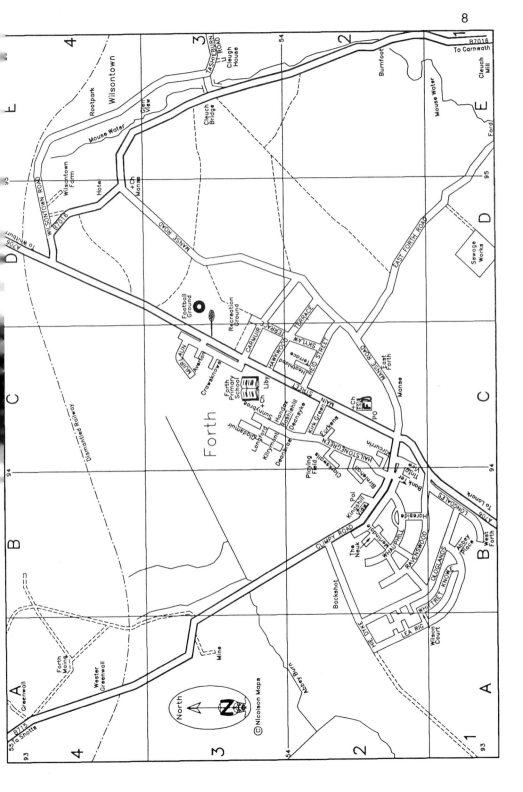

ASHGILL

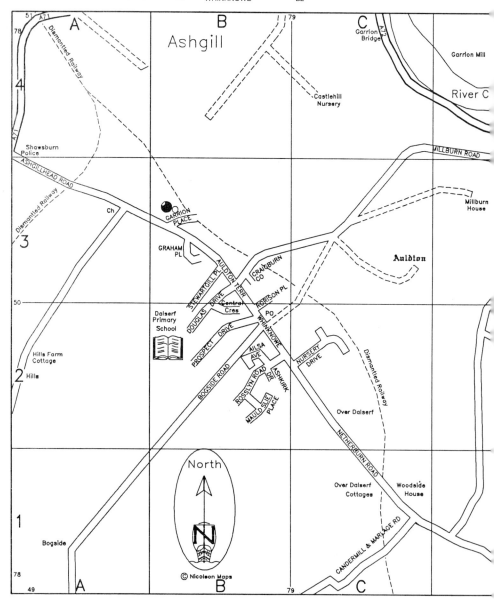

© Nicolson Maps

51
80

4
Dalserf

KIRK ROAD

A72
To Lanark

MANSE BRAE

3

50

Howlethole

2

1

80
49

STRATHAVEN

ABBOTSFORD CRES	A4
APPLEGARTH ROAD	A2
ARRAN COURT	C2
ASHKIRK ROAD	C4
ASPEN PLACE	D4
AULDGAVEL	B2
AVENEL CRESCENT	D4
AVONDALE STREET	C4
BANKFOOT PLACE	B5
BARBUSH PLACE	D3
BARN STREET	C3
BEECHWOOD COURT	D4
BIRCHFIELD PLACE	A2
BOWLING GREEN RD	B2
BRAEHEAD COURT	D3
BRIDGE STREET	C3
BROOK SREET	C4
BROOMFIELD ROAD	D1
BURN BRIDGE COURT	C1
BURN BRIDGE DRIVE	C1
BURNSHILL STREET	C1
CAIRNLEA ROAD	B2
CAMERON DRIVE	B3
CASTLE COURT (4)	C2
CASTLE STREET	C3
CASTLEVIEW	C2
CASTLEVIEW ROAD	A2
CEDAR PLACE	B2
CHAPEL ROAD	C3
CHERYTREE PLACE	C4
COCHRANE STREET	C3
COLDSTREAM DRIVE	C5
COLINHILL ROAD	B2
COMMERCIAL ROAD	D3
COMMON GREEN	C3
CORNEYS CLOSE (1)	C2
CRAWFORD STREET	B3
CROFTHEAD STREET	B2
CROSSHILL AVENUE	B2
CROSSHILL CRES	B3
CROSSHILL ROAD	B2
CULLIN PARK GROVE	B3
DARVEL ROAD	A2
DOUGLAS STREET	D1
DOVECASTLE DRIVE	C2
DUNAVON CRESCENT	B2
DUNAVON PARK	D3
DUNLOP COURT	C2
DUNLOP STREET	B2
EAGLESFIELD CRES	A2
FAILFORD ROAD	D4
FERNLEA ROAD	C4
FINNART PLACE	B2
GAS CLOSE (2)	C2
GATESHAW WYND	C4
GEORGE ALLAN PL	B4
GIFFEN PLACE	A3
GLASGOW ROAD	B5
GLASSFORD ROAD	D3
GLENAVON STREET	C1
GOODBUSH HILL	C2
GOODSBURN ROAD	C2
GREEN STREET	C3
GREYSTONE PLACE	D4
HAMILTON ROAD	D5
HAPTON VIEW	C5
HAWTHORN ROAD	B2
HAZELWOOD ROAD	A2
HIGHFIELD ROAD	A2
HILLS ROAD	D3
HOGAN DRIVE	C4
HOLM STREET	C3
KIBBLESTANE PLACE	A3
KIRK STREET	C2
KIRKHILL ROAD	A3
KIRKLAND PARK	A3
KIRKLAND PK AVE	B3
KYPE-VIEW	C2
LESMAHAGOW ROAD	D2
LETHAME GARDENS	B3
LETHAME ROAD	A3
LINDEN WALK	A2
LOCHABER ROAD	A2
LOUDON STREET	C3
MAIDENBURN GROVE	C4
MAIN STREET	C2
MAPLE COURT	C3
MARCHMONT GDNS	D4
MEADOWBANK AVE	C4
MIDCROFT PLACE	B2
MIDDLERIG	C2
MILLHOLM ROAD	C2
MOSS ROAD	C2
MUIRKIRK ROAD	B2
MUIRSIDE ROAD	C2
NEIDPATH PL	C4
NEWTON COURT	C2
NEWTON ROAD	C2
NORTH STREET	C3
NUTBERRY PLACE	A3
OAKLANDS	C4
ORCHARD GARDENS	C4
OVERTON AVENUE	C5
OVERTON PARK	D4
OVERTON ROAD	C4
OVERWOOD PLACE	D3
PALMER CRESCENT	C4
PARK CRESCENT	C4
PARK VIEW	C3
PINEWOOD WALK	C4
POWMILLON COURT	C5
PRIMROSE PLACE	C4
RAVENSWOOD ROAD	D4
REED STREET	C4
RIGHEAD PLACE	B2
ROKEBY CRESCENT	A4
ROSEBANK GARDENS	A2
ROWAN WALK	A2
RYELAND STREET	B2
SANDHEAD ROAD	A2
SOUTHEND COURT	D2
SOUTHEND DRIVE	D2
SOUTHEND GROVE	D2
SOUTHFIELD CRES	B2
SPRINGFIELD PL	D4
STANEHOLM ROAD	D4
STATION ROAD	C2
STONEHOUSE ROAD	D3
STRAIT CLOSE (3)	C2
THE WARD	C3
THOMSON STREET	C2
THORNWOOD ROAD	A2
THREESTANES RD	B4
TODSHILL STREET	C2
TOWNHEAD STREET	B2
TUKALO COURT	D5
TUKALO DRIVE	D5
TURNBULL COURT	D4
TURNBULL WAY	C4
VIEWMOUNT	C4
VIEWMOUNT CRES	C4
WATERSIDE STREET	C3
WATERYETT LOAN	A3
WEIRS GATE	C3
WELL BRAE	C2
WELLBRAE DRIVE	C4
WESTBARNS ROAD	C4
WHITESHAW VIEW	C5
WOODHILL ROAD	C4
WOODSIDE WALK	A2
YOUNG STREET	D3

Whiteshawgate 71 E 46

North

N

© Nicolson Maps

milton Road
Ind Est

East Overton

aehead
ourt

GLASSFORD ROAD

YOUNG ST

HILLS ROAD

GREYSTONE PL

SPRINGFIELD PLACE

Dismantled Railway

To Stonehouse
A71

Dismantled Railway

Southend Court

n Cottages
Gallowhill

Avonpark

To Blackwood
B7086

D 71 E

5

4

45

3

2

44

1

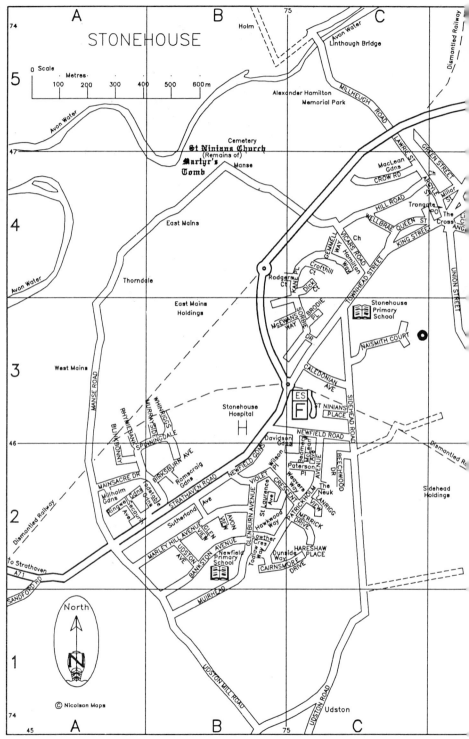

STONEHOUSE

ANGLE STREET	D4
ARGYLE STREET	C4
AVON VIEW	B2
BANKSTON AVENUE	B2
BEAMERS WALK	C2
BEECHWOOD DR	C2
BIRKSBURN AVE	B2
BLINKBONNY	A3
BOGHALL STREET	D4
BRODIE PLACE	C3
CAIRNSMORE DR	B2
CALEDONIAN AVE	C3
CAMNETHAN ST	D4
CANDER AVENUE	E5
CANDERMILL ROAD	E5
CROFTHILL CT	C4
CROW ROAD	C4
DAVIDSON GDNS	B2
DICK COURT	C4
DUNSIDE WAY	B2
GEMMELL WAY	C4
GLEN VIEW	B2
GLENBURN AVE	B2
GREEN STREET	D4
HAMILTON WAY	C4
HARESHAW PLACE	C2
HAWKWOOD WAY	B2
HILL ROAD	C4
KANE PLACE	C4
KING STREET	C4
KIRK STREET	D4
LANRIGG VIEW	C2
LAWRIE STREET	C5
LOCHART PLACE	D5
LOCKHART STREET	D5
LOWTHER CRES	B2
MACLEAN GDNS	C4
MAINSACRE DR	A2
MANSE ROAD	A3
MARLEY HILL AVE	B2
MCEWANS WAY	B3
MCLEAN AVENUE	C2
MERRICK DRIVE	C2
MILLAR STREET	D4
MILLHEUGH RD	C5
MILLHOLM GDNS	A2
MUIRHEAD	B1
MURRAY DRIVE	E4
MURRAYSIDE	B3
NAISMITH COURT	C3
NEW STREET	D4
NEWFIELD GDNS	B2
NEWFIELD ROAD	C3
PATERSON PL	C2
PATRICKHOLM AVE	C2
QUEEN STREET	C4
RAMSCRAIG GDNS	B2
RHYMIEBANK	A3
RINGWELL GDNS	A2
RODGERS CT	B4
SANDFORD ROAD	A1
SECAURIN AVE	A2
SIDEHEAD ROAD	C3
SORBIE DRIVE	C3
SPINNINGDALE	A2
SPITAL ROAD	E2
ST LAURENCE AVE	B2
ST NINIANS PL	C3
STRATHAVEN ROAD	B2
SUTHERLAND AVE	B2
THE CROSS	D4
THE NEUK	C2
TODLAW WAY	B2
TODSTABLE GDNS	A2
TOWNHEAD ST	C4
TRONGATE	C4
UDSTON AVENUE	B2
UDSTON MILL RD	B1
UDSTON ROAD	C1
UNION STREET	D4
VICARS ROAD	C4
VIOLET CRESCENT	B2
WATSON AVENUE	E4
WATSTONE ROAD	D4
WEAVERS WAY	C2
WELL BRAE	C4
WHINRIGGS	B3
WILSON PLACE	B2

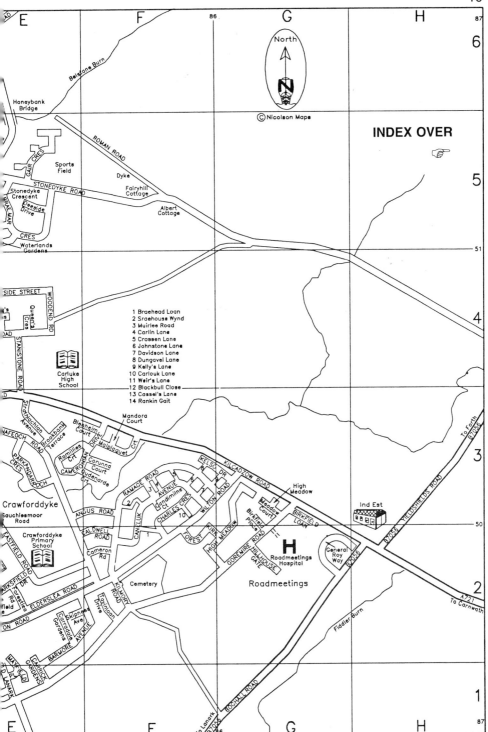

North

Ⓒ Nicolson Maps

INDEX OVER ☞

1 Braehead Loan
2 Sraehouse Wynd
3 Muirlee Road
4 Carlin Lane
5 Crossen Lane
6 Johnstone Lane
7 Davidson Lane
8 Dungavel Lane
9 Kelly's Lane
10 Carlouk Lane
11 Weir's Lane
12 Blackbull Close
13 Cassel's Lane
14 Rankin Gait

Crawforddyke

Roadmeetings

Cemetery

CARLUKE

AIRDRIE ROAD	C6	ELMBANK STREET	E2	LOCKHART STREET	D4	STRATHLACHLAN AVE	E3
ALLAN AVENUE	C5	ESCART ROAD	D5	LOCHPARK AVENUE	D2	TANTALLON COURT	C5
ANDREW PLACE	C5	FLEMING COURT	C3	LUGGIE ROAD	C5	TARBERT PLACE	E3
ANGUS ROAD	F3	FOREST KIRK	F2	MALPLAQUET CT	F3	TAYINLOAN DRIVE	F2
AQUILA WAY	B4	FORESTLEA RD	E2	MANDORA COURT	F3	THOMSON STREET	D4
ARNUM GARDENS	D3	GAIR CRESCENT	E5	MARIGOLD WAY	D2	THORNLEA STREET	E2
ARNUM PLACE	D3	GAIR ROAD	E6	MARKET PLACE	D4	THREAVE COURT	C5
ARRAN GARDENS	D2	GASWORKS ROAD	A5	MARKET ROAD	D4	UNION STREET	D3
AVON AVENUE	C4	GENERAL ROY WAY	G2	MAULDSLIE ROAD	A4	UNITAS CRESCENT	C2
BARMORE AVENUE	E2	GIGHA GARDENS	E2	MAYFIELD GDNS	E1	VICTORIA AVENUE	C3
BARR'S LANE	D5	GILLBANK AVENUE	B4	MAYFIELD PLACE	E1	VIOLET GARDENS	C4
BEECHFIELD DRIVE	E2	GLAMIS AVENUE	D4	MEADOW COURT	G3	WATERLANDS GDNS	E5
BELSTANE GATE	E5	GLENAFEOCH ROAD	E3	MELVILLE PLACE	C4	WEIGHHOUSE ROAD	C5
BELSTANE PARK	D5	GLENBURN TERRACE	C2	MIDDLEHOUSE CT	B4	WEIR'S LANE (11)	F4
BELSTANE ROAD	E5	GLENCOE ROAD	E2	MILL ROAD	C3	WEST AVENUE	B3
BENTY'S LANE	D2	GLENDERMOTT CT	D5	MILLER STREET	E4	WESTERHOUSE CT	B4
BIRKFIELD LOAN	G3	GLENMAVIS CRES	E3	MILTON CRESCENT	D3	WHITEHILL CRES	D5
BIRKFIELD PLACE	G3	GOREMIRE ROAD	G2	MILTON ROAD	D2	WHITESHAW AVE	B3
BLACKBULL CL (12)	F3	GOREMIRE ROAD	E1	MILTON STREET	C4	WHITESHAW DRIVE	B4
BLENHEIM COURT	E3	GOWANSIDE PLACE	B4	MOORSIDE STREET	E4	WILTON ROAD	F3
BLUEBELL WAY	D2	GREENBANK TERR	D4	MOSS SIDE AVENUE	B4	WILTON ROAD	E2
BOGHALL ROAD	F1	GREENFIELD ROAD	D5	MOUNT STEWART ST	C4	WINDSOR COURT	D4
BOTHWELL ROAD	C5	HALLCRAIG PLACE	B4	MUIRLEE ROAD (3)	F4	WINDSOR QUAD	D4
BRAEHEAD LOAN (1)	F4	HAMILTON STREET	D3	NEEDLE GREEN	D4	WISTERIA LANE	D2
BRAEMAR CRESCENT	E5	HEADSMUIR AVENUE	B4	NEIDPATH ROAD	C5	WOODEND ROAD	D5
BRIDGEND VIEW	D3	HEATHER ROW	C6	NEWBARNS STREET	D5	YIELDSHIELDS RD	H3
BROOKBANK TERR	E3	HEMMINGEN COURT	C5	NEWBRIDGE END	D3	YVETOT COURT	C5
BROWN STREET	D5	HIGH MEADOW	G3	NEWLANDS TERRACE	D4		
BURN ROAD	D5	HIGH MEADOW	F2	NIMMO PLACE	C5		
BURNBANK BRAES	D3	HIGH MILL ROAD	E4	NORTH AVENUE	B4		
BURTON LANE	C4	HIGH STREET	D4	NURSERY COURT	C5	**MAP PAGE 16**	
BUSHELHEAD ROAD	D1	HILLFOOT TERRACE	E3	OLD BRIDGEND	D3		
CAIRNBAN COURT	D5	HILLHEAD AVENUE	E4	OLD LANARK ROAD	E2		
CAIRNEYMOUNT RD	E4	HILLHOUSE GATE	G2	OLD LANARK ROAD	E1		
CAIRNHILL COURT	D4	HOLM STREET	C4	OLD WISHAW ROAD	B6		
CALDWELL ROAD	F2	HONEYBANK CRES	E5	OLD WISHAW ROAD	C5		
CAMERON ROAD	F2	HOPE STREET	E4	ORCHARD STREET	D3		
CAMERONIAN DRIVE	E3	HOZIER STREET	D4	ORION WAY	B4		
CANDIMILNE CT	F3	HYACINTH WAY	D2	OUDENARDE COURT	F3		
CANELUK AVENUE	F3	HYNDSHAW ROAD	D5	PARK AVENUE	D5		
CARLIN LANE (4)	F4	ISLAY GARDENS	D2	PARK CIRCUS	D5		
CARLOUK LANE (10)	F4	IVANHOE COURT	B3	PARK LANE	C3		
CARNWATH ROAD	E3	JACKSON PLACE	C5	PARK STREET	C3		
CARRADALE GDNS	E2	JAMES STREET	D3	PARKANDARROCH CR	E3		
CARRANBUIE ROAD	D5	JASMINE WAY	C2	PEACOCK LOAN	D5		
CARRICK GARDENS	E1	JOHN STREET	D3	PEGASUS AVENUE	C4		
CARTLAND AVE	D2	JOHNSTONE LN (6)	F4	PRIMROSE WAY	C2		
CASSEL'S LANE (13)	F3	JONQUIL WAY	D2	QUEEN'S CRESCENT	E4		
CASSELS STREET	D3	JURA GARDENS	E2	RAMAGE ROAD	F3		
CASTLEHILL ROAD	C6	KELLY'S LANE (9)	F4	RAMILLIES COURT	E3		
CHAPEL STREET	D4	KELSO DRIVE	F3	RANKIN GAIT (14)	F3		
CHARLES CRESCENT	F3	KENILWORTH COURT	B3	RANKIN STREET	D4		
CHESTNUT GROVE	D3	KENMORE WAY	D5	REDHOUSE LANE	D5		
CHURCH LANE	D3	KILCADZOW ROAD	G3	ST LUKE'S AVENUE	C2		
CLYDE STREET	C4	KILMARTIN LANE	D5	SANDY ROAD	D5		
COLUMBINE WAY	D2	KILMORY GARDENS	E5	SAUCHIESMOOR RD	E3		
CORUNNA COURT	F3	KILMORY ROAD	F2	SCHOOL LANE	C4		
CRAIGNETHAN ROAD	C5	KING'S CRESCENT	E4	SHAND LANE	D5		
CRATHIE COURT	C5	KINTYRE WYND	D5	SHIELDHILL ROAD	D2		
CROSSEN LANE (5)	F4	KIRK ROAD	C4	SKIPNESS AVENUE	E2		
DAVIDSON LANE (7)	F4	KIRK STREET	C4	SOUTH AVENUE	C4		
DEESIDE DRIVE	E5	KIRKSTYLE AVENUE	C3	SPRINGFIELD CRES	D2		
DEVON GARDENS	C4	KIRKTON AVENUE	C3	SRAEHOUSE WYND(2)	F4		
DOUGLAS STREET	C4	KIRKTON COURT	C3	STANISTONE ROAD	E4		
DUNARD COURT	C5	KIRKTON STREET	D3	STATION ROAD	C3		
DUNGAVEL LANE (8)	F4	LAGAN ROAD	D3	STEVENSON STREET	C4		
EAST AVENUE	B4	LANARK ROAD	D1	STEWART STREET	C4		
EASTFIELD ROAD	E2	LANGSHAW CRES	D4	STIRLING ROAD	C6		
ELDERSLEA ROAD	E2	LARKSFIELD DR	E2	STONEDYKE CRES	E5		
		LARKSPUR WAY	D2	STONEDYKE ROAD	E5		
		LAVENDER LANE	C2	STONEFIELD GDNS	D5		

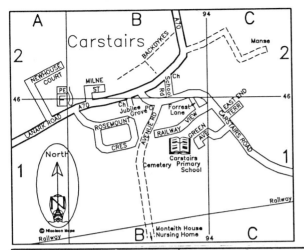

CARSTAIRS

AVENUE ROAD	B1
BACKDYKES	B2
CARSTAIRS ROAD	C1
EAST END TERR	C1
FORREST LANE	B1
GREEN AVENUE	B1
JUBILEE GROVE	B1
LANARK ROAD	A1
MILNE STREET	B2
NEWHOUSE CT	A2
RAILWAY VIEW	B1
ROSEMOUNT CRES	B1
SCHOOL ROAD	B2

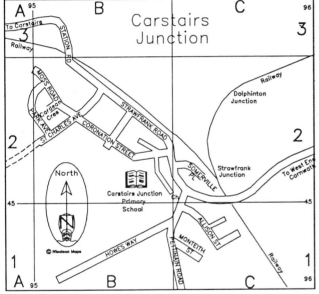

CARSTAIRS JUNCTION

ALLISON STREET	C1
CARDEAN CRES	B2
CORONATION ST	B2
HOWES WAY	B1
MONTEITH ST	C1
MOSS ROAD	B2
PARK AVE	A2
PETTINAIN ROAD	B1
SOMERVILLE PL	C2
ST CHARLES AVE	B2
STATION ROAD	B3
STRAWFRANK RD	B2

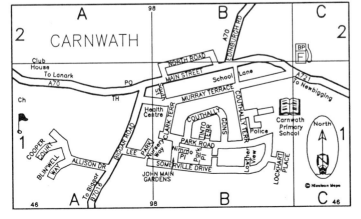

CARNWATH

ALLISON DRIVE	A1
BIGGAR ROAD	A1
BLIN'WELL WAY	A1
CLARK TERRACE	B1
COOPER COURT	A1
COUTHALLY GDNS	B1
COUTHALLY TERR	B1
EDINBURGH RD	B2
JOHN MAIN GDNS	A1
LEE PARK	A1
LOCKHART PLACE	B1
LOWTHER VIEW	B1
MAIN STREET	B1
MURRAY TERRACE	B1
NIMMO PLACE	B1
NORTH ROAD	B1
NURSERY WAY	B1
PARK PLACE	B1
PARK ROAD	B1
SCHOOL LANE	B1
SOMERVILLE DR	B1
SOUTH STREET	B1
TINTO TERRACE	B1

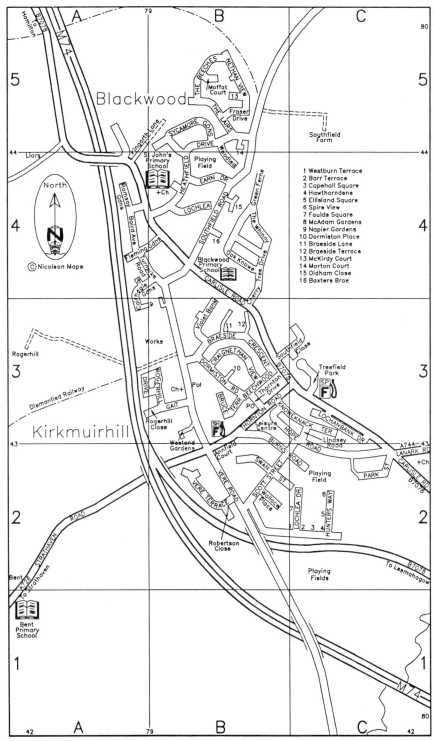

19

Blackwood

Kirkmuirhill

North
N
© Nicolson Maps

1 Westburn Terrace
2 Barr Terrace
3 Capehall Square
4 Hawthorndene
5 Ellisland Square
6 Spire View
7 Faulds Square
8 McAdam Gardens
9 Napier Gardens
10 Dormiston Place
11 Braeside Lane
12 Braeside Terrace
13 McKirdy Court
14 Morton Court
15 Oldham Close
16 Baxters Brae

BLACKWOOD

ANNFIELD COURT	B2
BAIRD AVENUE	A4
BARR TERRACE (2)	C4
BAXTERS BRAE (16)	C4
BEECHWOOD	B3
BRAESIDE CRES	B3
BRAESIDE LANE (11)	C4
BRAESIDE TERR (12)	C4
BRUCE TERRACE	B3
BURNS ROAD	B2
CAIRNEGIE GDNS	A4
CAPEHALL SQ (3)	C4
CARLISLE ROAD	B4
CARLISLE ROAD	C2
CHERRY TREE DRIVE	B4
CRAIGNETHAN VIEW	B3
DORMISTON PL (10)	C4
DORMISTON ROAD	B3
EARN DRIVE	B4
ELLISLAND SQ (5)	C4
FAULDS SQUARE (7)	C4
FLEMING GARDENS	B4
FRASER DRIVE	B5
GREEN FERNS	B4
HAWTHORNDENE (4)	C4
HEATHFIELD DRIVE	B4
HOPE ROAD	C3
HUNTERS WAY	C2
KINGARTH LANE	A5
KNOWEKNACK TERR	C3
LANARK ROAD	C2
LINDSEY ROAD	C3
LOCHANBANK DRIVE	C3
LOCHLEA	B4
LOCHLEA DRIVE	C2
MCADAM GDNS (8)	C4
MCKIRDY COURT (13)	C4
MOFFAT COURT	B5
MORTON COURT (14)	C4
NAPIER GARDENS (9)	C4
NETHAN VIEW	B5
OAK KNOWE	B4
OLDHAM CLOSE (15)	C4
PARK STREET	C2
RAMSAY GARDENS	A4
ROBERTSON CLOSE	B2
ROGERHILL CLOSE	B3
ROGERHILL DRIVE	B3
ROGERHILL GAIT	B3
SCOTT STREET	B2
SOUTHFIELD CLOSE	B3
SOUTHFIELD ROAD	B4
SPIRE VIEW (6)	C4
STRATHAVEN ROAD	A2
SWAN STREET	B2
SYCAMORE GDNS	B5
THE BEECHES	B5
THE LAIRS	B5
THE WHINNY	B4
THORNTON DRIVE	B3
THORNTON ROAD	B3
TREEFIELD PARK	C3
TURNPIKE ROAD	A4
VERE ROAD	B2
VERE TERRACE	B2
VIOLET BANK	B3
WALLACE PLACE	B3
WESTBURN TERR (1)	C4
WESTEND GARDENS	B2
WOODLEA	B4

LANARK

ABBOTSFORD TERR	F4
AITKEN PLACE (1)	D3
ALBANY DRIVE	E3
ARMADALE ROAD	F4
BANKHEAD TERRACE	D2
BANNATYNE STREET	D4
BATTISMAINS	E4
BAXTER LANE	D4
BELL'S WYND	F5
BELLFIELD RD	D6
BENDIGO PLACE	D4
BERNARD'S CT (17)	D2
BERNARD'S WY (16)	D3
BIRKS PLACE	D5
BLOOMGATE	D4
BONNET ROAD	D4
BONNINGTON AVE	D3
BRAEDALE ROAD	D5
BRAIDFUTE	F5
BRAXFIELD ROAD	D3
BRAXFIELD ROW	C2
BRAXFIELD TERR	C2
BRIARBANK AVENUE	D3
BROOMGATE	C4
BULL'S CLOSE (8)	D3
BYRETOWN ROAD	B3
CAITHNESS ROW	D2
CAMERONIAN COURT	F5
CARMICHAEL COURT	F4
CARSTAIRS ROAD	G5
CARTLAND VIEW	C5
CASTLEGATE	C3
CHAPLAND ROAD	D5
CLEGHORN AVENUE	E5
CLEGHORN ROAD	D5
CLYDE CRESCENT	E5
COUNTY DRIVE	F3
CROSS KEY'S CL (5)	D3
CROSSLAW AVENUE	F3
DEAD MAN'S LANE	E3
DELVES COURT	D4
DELVES PARK	D4
DELVES ROAD	D3
DENNISTON PL (14)	D3
DOUBLE ROW	C2
DOUGLAS TERRACE	C4
DOVECOT LANE	D4
DROVE ROAD	G4
DUNCAN CLOSE (4)	D3
EAST FAULDS RD	G5
FORREST ROAD	E5
FORSYTH COURT	F4
FRIAR'S DENE	C4
FRIAR'S LANE	C4
FRIAR'S WYND	C4
FRIARSFIELD ROAD	C4
GALLOWHILL ROAD	D4
GILROY CLOSE	F5
GLASGOW ROAD	B4
GLEBE COURT	D4
GLEBE DRIVE	D4
GRANGE COURT	C5
GREENSIDE CL (2)	D3
GREENSIDE LANE	D4
GREYSTONE BAUKS	C4
HALL PLACE	D4
HARDACRES	D5
HIGH STREET	D4
HIGHBURGH AVENUE	E4
HIGHBURGH COURT	E4
HILLHOUSE FM GATE	B5
HILLHOUSE FARM RD	B4
HOME STREET	F3
HONEYMAN CRES	F4
HOPE STREET	D4
HORSE MARKET	E4
HOSPITLAND DRIVE	F4
HOWACRE	C5

HUNTER'S CLOSE (7)	D3
HYNDFORD PLACE	C4
HYNDFORD ROAD	E3
JERVIS WOOD ROAD	D4
KENILWORTH ROAD	E4
KILDARE DRIVE	E4
KILDARE PLACE	E4
KILDARE ROAD	E4
KINGSMYRE	F4
KIRKFIELD ROAD	A4
KIRKFIELDBANK BRAE	B4
KIRKLANDS ROAD	E3
LADYACRE ROAD	E4
LAKE AVENUE	G2
LANARK ROAD	A6
LAVEROCKHALL	E5
LEECH FORD	E5
LIMPETLAW	E5
LINDSAY LOAN	F5
LINTHILL	E6
LOCHART DRIVE	C5
LONG ROW	C2
LYTHGOW WAY	F5
MAINS COURT	F6
MANSE ROAD	C4
MARKET COURT	D4
MARKET END	C4
MARR'S WYND	F5
MCKENZIE'S CL (9)	D3
MELVINHALL ROAD	D5
MOORPARK CT (18)	D2
MOUSEBANK LANE	C4
MOUSEBANK ROAD	C5
MOUSEMILL ROAD	A5
NEMPHLAT HILL	C5
NEW BUILDINGS	D2
NEW LANARK ROAD	D2
NEWLANDS STREET	F3
NORTH FAULDS RD	G5
NORTH VENNEL	D4
NURSERY BLDGS	D2
PARK DRIVE	B4
PARK PLACE	C4
PORTLAND PLACE	E4
POTTERS WYND	F5
QUARRYKNOWE	D5
RAMOTH	A4
RENWICK PLACE	F5
RHYBER AVENUE	E5
RIDGEPARK DRIVE	C5
RITCHIE'S CL (6)	D3
RIVERSIDE ROAD	A4
ROSEDALE STREET	C2
RUSSELL ROAD	E5
SCARLETMUIR	C5
SHIELDS LOAN	C5
SHIRLEY'S CL (3)	D3
SILVERDALE CT (11)	D3
SILVERDALE CRES	C4
SMIDDY COURT	D4
SMYLLUM PARK	F4
SMYLLUM ROAD	F4
SOUTH VENNEL	D4
SPRINGFIELD GDNS	C5
ST KENTIGERN'S RD	E5
ST LEONARD STREET	E4
ST LEONARD STREET	F5
ST LEONARD'S ROAD	E4
ST MUNGO'S	D3
ST NICHOLAS ROAD	E5
ST NINIAN'S	E6
ST PATRICK'S COURT	C4
ST PATRICK'S LANE	C4
ST PATRICK'S ROAD	C4
ST TEILING	E6
ST VINCENT PLACE	E4
STAIKHILL	C5
STANMORE AVENUE	E5
STANMORE CRES	F5
STANMORE ROAD	G5
STEY BRAE	C6

STUART DRIVE	E5
SUNNYSIDE ROAD	A5
THE BEECHES	E2
THE BUTTS	C3
THE GLEBE	C4
THE MARCHES	E5
THE RODDING	E5
THOMPSON'S CL (10)	D3
TINTO COURT (19)	D2
WALLACE WAY	F4
WATERLOO DRIVE	D5
WATERLOO ROAD	D5
WAVERLEY CRES	F5
WEAVER'S WALK	D3
WELL ROAD	D3
WELLGATE	D4
WELLGATEHEAD	D3
WELLHEAD CL (12)	D3
WELLHEAD CT (13)	D3
WELLINGTON TERR	C5
WELLWOOD AVENUE	E5
WEST NEMPHLAR RD	A5
WEST FAULDS RD	G5
WEST PORT	C4
WESTCOTT PLACE	F5
WHEATLAND DRIVE	C5
WHEATLANDSIDE	C5
WHEATPARK ROAD	C4
WHITE'S NEUK (15)	D3
WHITEHILL CRES	C4
WHITEHILL TERR	C4
WHITELEES ROAD	F3
WIDE CLOSE	D4
WOODSTOCK AVE	F4
WOODSTOCK DRIVE	E4
WOODSTOCK ROAD	E4
YOUNG ROAD	G5
YVETOT AVENUE	E4

MAP PAGE 21

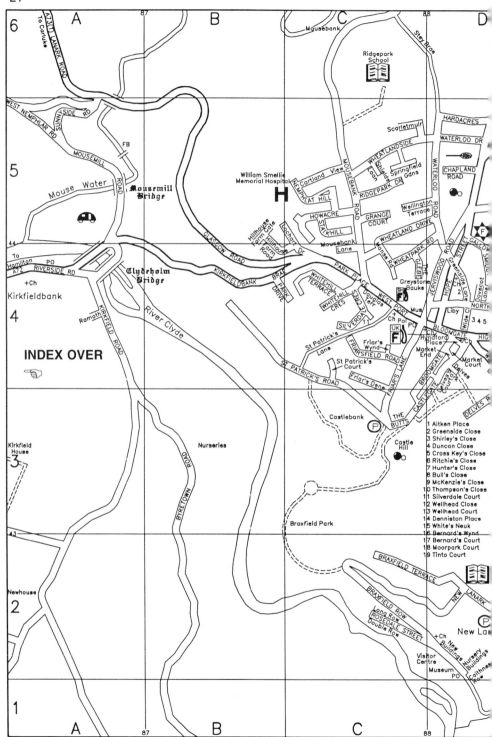

INDEX OVER 👉

1 Aitken Place
2 Greenside Close
3 Shirley's Close
4 Duncan Close
5 Cross Key's Close
6 Ritchie's Close
7 Hunter's Close
8 Bull's Close
9 McKenzie's Close
10 Thompson's Close
11 Silverdale Court
12 Wellhead Close
13 Wellhead Court
14 Denniston Place
15 White's Neuk
16 Bernard's Wynd
17 Bernard's Court
18 Moorpark Court
19 Tinto Court

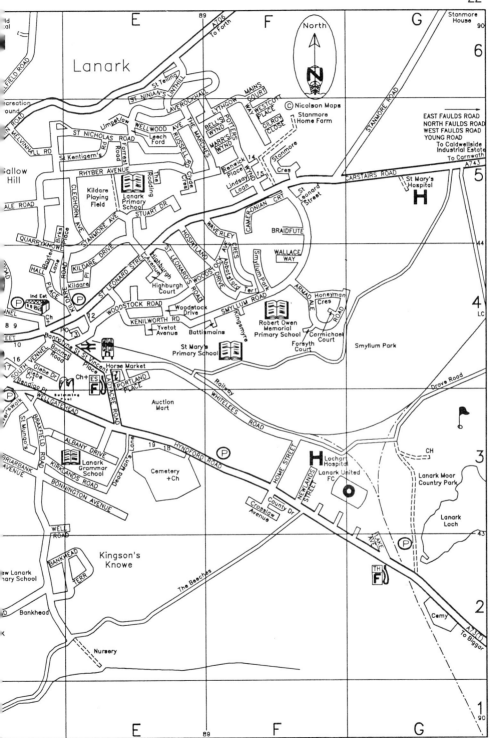

Lanark

North

© Nicolson Maps

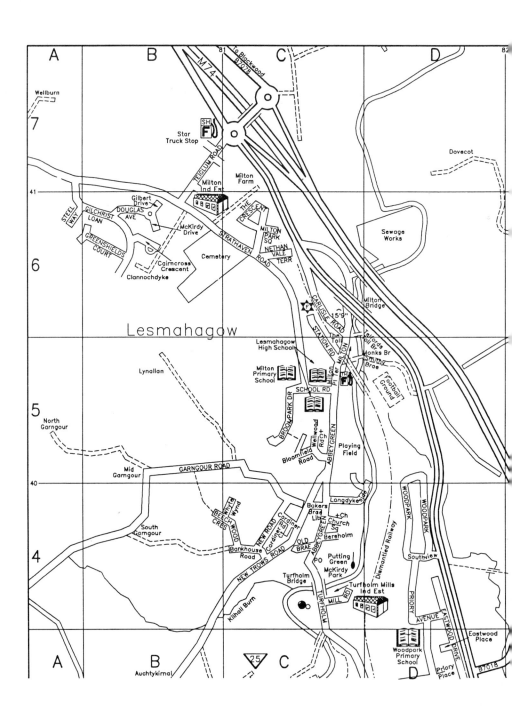

LESMAHAGOW

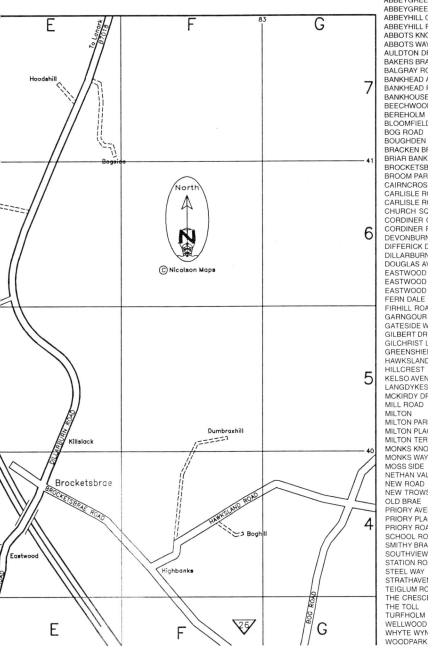

ABBEY GREEN	C5
ABBEYGREEN	C4
ABBEYGREEN ROAD	D3
ABBEYHILL CRES	D3
ABBEYHILL ROAD	D2
ABBOTS KNOWE	D3
ABBOTS WAY	D3
AULDTON DRIVE	D2
BAKERS BRAE	C4
BALGRAY ROAD	D2
BANKHEAD AVENUE	D3
BANKHEAD ROAD	D3
BANKHOUSE ROAD	C4
BEECHWOOD CRES	B4
BEREHOLM	C4
BLOOMFIELD ROAD	C5
BOG ROAD	G3
BOUGHDEN WAY	D2
BRACKEN BRAE	D2
BRIAR BANK	D2
BROCKETSBRAE RD	E4
BROOM PARK DRIVE	C5
CAIRNCROSS CRES	B6
CARLISLE ROAD	F1
CARLISLE ROAD	C6
CHURCH SQUARE	C4
CORDINER COURT	C4
CORDINER ROAD	C4
DEVONBURN ROAD	F3
DIFFERICK DRIVE	D2
DILLARBURN ROAD	E5
DOUGLAS AVENUE	B6
EASTWOOD DRIVE	D4
EASTWOOD PLACE	D3
EASTWOOD ROAD	E3
FERN DALE	D2
FIRHILL ROAD	D2
GARNGOUR ROAD	B5
GATESIDE WALK	D2
GILBERT DRIVE	B6
GILCHRIST LOAN	B6
GREENSHIELDS CT	B6
HAWKSLAND ROAD	F4
HILLCREST	D2
KELSO AVENUE	D2
LANGDYKESIDE	C4
MCKIRDY DRIVE	B6
MILL ROAD	C4
MILTON	C5
MILTON PARK SQ	C6
MILTON PLACE	C5
MILTON TERRACE	C5
MONKS KNOWE	D2
MONKS WAY	D2
MOSS SIDE	D2
NETHAN VALE TERR	C6
NEW ROAD	C4
NEW TROWS ROAD	C4
OLD BRAE	C4
PRIORY AVENUE	D4
PRIORY PLACE	D3
PRIORY ROAD	D3
SCHOOL ROAD	C5
SMITHY BRAE	D5
SOUTHVIEW	D4
STATION ROAD	C5
STEEL WAY	A6
STRATHAVEN ROAD	C6
TEIGLUM ROAD	B7
THE CRESCENT	C6
THE TOLL	C5
TURFHOLM	C4
WELLWOOD ROAD	C5
WHYTE WYND	C4
WOODPARK	D4

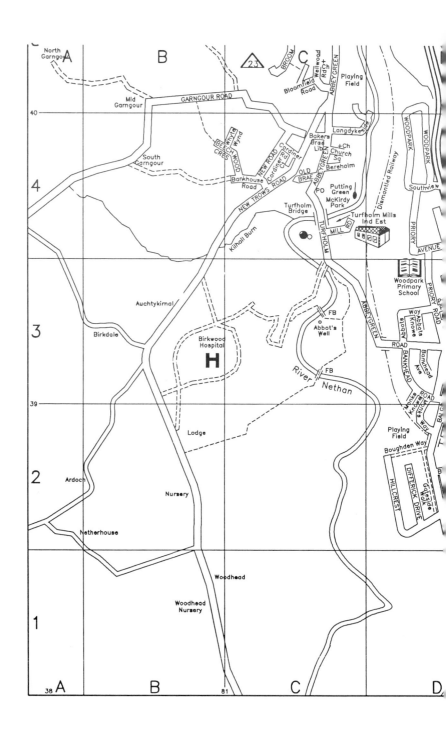

27

RIGSIDE

AYR ROAD	A1
BEECHGROVE ST	B2
BROOMFIELD STREET	B2
CRAIGLE STREET	B2
DOUGLAS WATER RD	B2
DOUGLASDALE ST	B2
LYONSIDE STREET	C2
MANSFIELD PLACE	A1
MOUNTSTUART ST	C2
MUIRFOOT ROAD	B1
NEWTONHEAD ROAD	B2
STUART TERRACE	C2
WHITESIDE STREET	C2

COALBURN

BEECHMOUNT AVE	C2
BELLFIELD ROAD	C2
BELVEDERE PLACE	B1
BRAEHEAD PLACE	B1
BRAEHEAD ROAD	B2
BURNSIDE PLACE	B2
COALBURN ROAD	B2
DUNN CRESCENT	B2
GARDEN STREET	B2
MANSE VIEW	B2
MIDDLEMUIR ROAD	A1
MIDFIELD ROAD	C2
MUIRBURN PLACE	B4
PARK STREET	C2
RAILWAY ROAD	B2
SCHOOL ROAD	B3
SHOULDERIGG PL	B3
SHOULDERIGG ROAD	A3

DOUGLAS

ADDISON DRIVE	A3
ADDISON GARDENS	B2
ADDISON PLACE	B2
ANGUS AVENUE	B2
AYR ROAD	B3
BELL'S WYND (5)	A2

BLACKWOOD COURT	A3
BLUE TOWER (4)	A2
BRAEHEAD	B3
BROWNHILL AVENUE	B2
BROWNHILL GDNS	B2
CLYDE ROAD (6)	A2
COLONEL'S ENTRY	B3
CORRIE'S CLOSE (3)	A2
CRABTREE STREET	B4
DALE STREET	B3
DOCTOR'S CLOSE (2)	A2
ELMBANK DRIVE (1)	A2
GATESIDE ROAD	B2
GLEBE AVENUE	B2
HAGSHAW TERRACE	B2
HAGSHAW VIEW	B2
HILL STREET	B3
KILNCROFT TERR	B3
KIRKGATE	B4
MAIN STREET	B3
MANSE VIEW TERR	B2
NURSERY AVENUE (7)	A2
PATHHEAD	A3
SPRINGHILL AVENUE	B2
SPRINGHILL ROAD	B3
SPRINGHILL STREET	B2
STATION ROAD	A2
THE LOANING	B3
WEAVER'S YARD	B3
WELLDALE STREET	B3

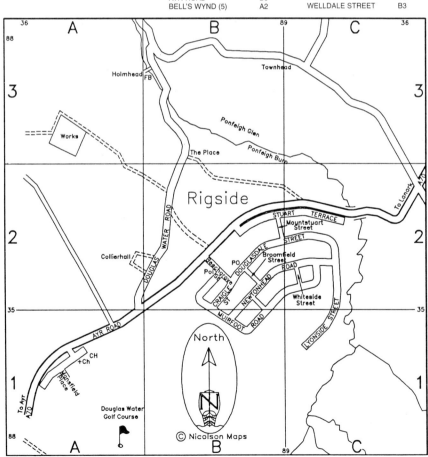

© Nicolson Maps

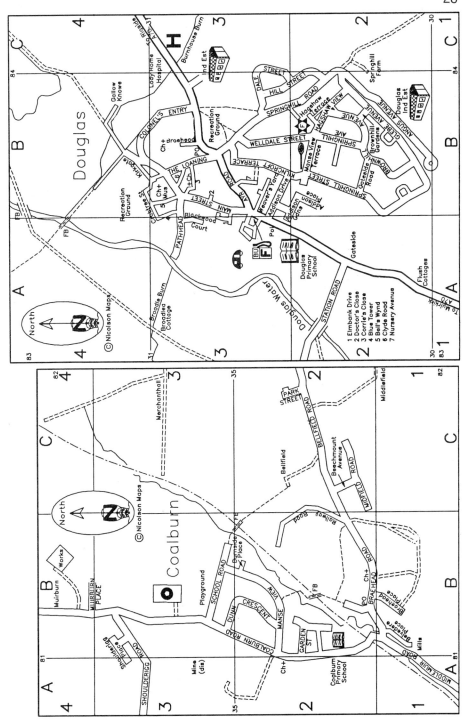

Douglas

1 Elmbank Drive
2 Doctor's Close
3 Corrie's Close
4 Blue Tower
5 Bell's Wynd
6 Clyde Road
7 Nursery Avenue

Coalburn

BIGGAR

		CARWOOD ROAD	C4	GUILDIES LOAN	D4	LANGVOUT GAIT	D4
		CASTLE YETT	B2	HIGH STREET	C3	LANGVOUT SQUARE	C3
ABATTOIR ROAD	C2	COLLIEHILL ROAD	D3	HOWIESON SQ (10)	A1	LEAFIELD ROAD	D4
ALBION COURT	C3	COULTER ROAD	B2	JAMES SQUARE (5)	A1	LINDSAYLANDS RD	A2
BALLGREEN ROAD	B2	CROFTFOOT TERR	B3	JOHN'S LOAN	C3	LODGE PARK	B2
BENCROFT AVENUE	C3	CROSS ROAD	C4	JOHNS STREET	C3	MANSE DRIVE	D3
BIGGAR MILL RD	B4	CROWN RIG (13)	A1	KIRKSTYLE	C3	MARSHALL'S CL (8)	A1
BOGHALL AVENUE	B2	DENE PARK	D3	KNOCK STREET	B3	MERCAT LOAN	C3
BOGHALL PARK	B2	EDINBURGH ROAD	D4	KNOCKBANK	B3	MID ROAD	D3
BOWLING GREEN LA	D4	FLEMING WAY	B2	KNOCKLEA	B3	MILLSTONE PARK	C3
BROUGHTON ROAD	D3	FOREKNOWE	C3	KNOCKLEA PLACE	B3	MITCHELL KNO (14)	A1
BROWNLIE'S CL (3)	A1	GAS WORKS RD (16)	A1	KNOCKSIDE	B3	MOAT COTTS (15)	A1
BRYDEN'S CLOSE (7)	A1	GEORGE SQ (12)	A1	LAMBIE'S CLOSE (4)	A1	NORTH BACK RD	C3
BURNSIDE TERRACE	B3	GIBSON'S CLOSE (2)	A1	LANGLEES ROAD	A3	NORTH CROFTS RD	C4
CARDON DRIVE	B2	GILBERT RAE CT (9)	A1	LANGVOUT COURT	C3	PARK PLACE	B3

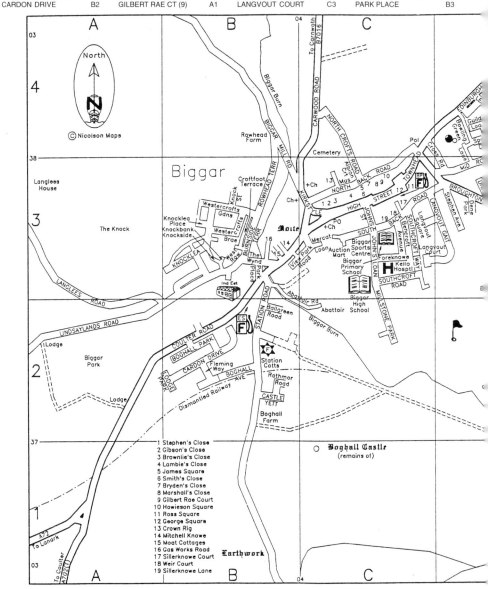

1 Stephen's Close
2 Gibson's Close
3 Brownlie's Close
4 Lambie's Close
5 James Square
6 Smith's Close
7 Bryden's Close
8 Marshall's Close
9 Gilbert Rae Court
10 Howieson Square
11 Ross Square
12 George Square
13 Crown Rig
14 Mitchell Knowe
15 Moat Cottages
16 Gas Works Road
17 Sillerknowe Court
18 Weir Court
19 Sillerknowe Lane

PARK ROAD	D3	STEPHEN'S CL (1)	A1
RATHMOR ROAD	B2	THE WYND	B3
ROSS SQUARE (11)	A1	TOWNHEAD	C3
ROWHEAD TERRACE	B3	VIEW PARK ROAD	C3
SILLERKNOWE CT(17)	A1	WEIR COURT (18)	A1
SILLERKNOWE LN (19)	A1	WEST ROW	B3
SMITH'S CLOSE (6)	A1	WESTERCROFTS BRAE	B3
SOUTH BACK RD	C3	WESTERCROFTS	
SOUTHCROFT ROAD	C3	GARDENS	B3
SOUTHCROFT WAY	C3		
SPRINGDALE DR	D4		
STANEHEAD PARK	D3		
STATION ROAD	B2		
STEPHEN AVENUE	D3		

ABINGTON

CARLISLE ROAD	B3
COLEBROOKE TERR	B2
EDINBURGH ROAD	B3
GLENGONNAR CRES	B2
HUNTERS COURT	B2
LEADHILLS ROAD	A1
MURDOSTOUN PL	A2
STATION ROAD	B2

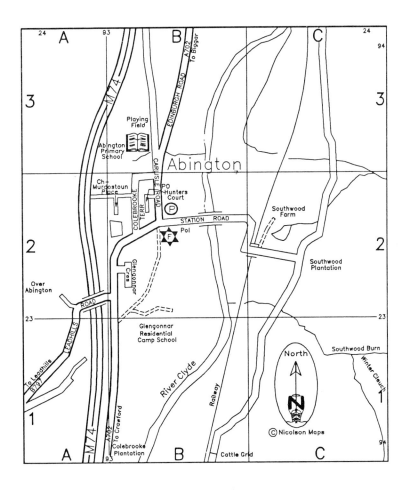